Claus Mayer

Non-Tariff Barriers to Agricultural Trade between Turkey and the EU

Anchor Compact

Mayer, Claus: Non-Tariff Barriers to Agricultural Trade between Turkey and the EU.
Hamburg, Anchor Academic Publishing 2014

Buch-ISBN: 978-3-95489-260-0
PDF-eBook-ISBN: 978-3-95489-760-5
Druck/Herstellung: Anchor Academic Publishing, Hamburg, 2014

Bibliografische Information der Deutschen Nationalbibliothek:
Die Deutsche Nationalbibliothek verzeichnet diese Publikation in der Deutschen Nationalbibliografie; detaillierte bibliografische Daten sind im Internet über http://dnb.d-nb.de abrufbar

Bibliographical Information of the German National Library:
The German National Library lists this publication in the German National Bibliography. Detailed bibliographic data can be found at: http://dnb.d-nb.de

Abstract

This thesis reviews the border effect approach as an application of gravity models of trade and different methods of including multilateral resistance terms (MRTs) in it. Some focus is laid on the endogeneity problem of the approach. In an empirical application of the approach, agricultural trade between Turkey and the EU is analysed; the effect of data pooling and aggregation is studied; the conversion of estimated border effects into ad-valorem tariff equivalents (AVEs) reveals the crucial importance of a reliable measure of the elasticity of substitution when trying to separate the effects of NTBs of the total effect of a border.

Keywords: Non-tariff barriers to trade; gravity model; border effect approach; agricultural trade; EU; Turkey; ad-valorem tariff equivalents;

Acknowledgements

First and foremost, I would like to thank my supervisor Prof. Dr. Martina Brockmeier for the unique opportunity to work on this topic and her continued support throughout the writing of this thesis. Her agreement to let me read and cite her unpublished work (Befus et al. 2012) enabled me to put my results into context.

I wish to express particular gratitude to M.Sc. Tanja Engelbert for her significant contributions to this thesis in the form of numerous discussions and constructive comments, which have greatly improved this work.

Further, I thank Prof. Dr. Harald Grethe for his time and resources involved in being the second supervisor of this thesis.

Moritz Stollovsky has put a great deal of time and motivation into proof-reading this thesis and has provided helpful suggestions for corrections and improvements, which I highly appreciate.

Finally, my special thanks go to my wife Ivana and our family for their ongoing support throughout the writing of this thesis and my entire Bachelor and Master Studies. I could not have made these achievements without you.

Contents

List of Tables

List of Abbreviations

CEPII	Centre d'Etudes Prospectives et d'Informations Internationales
EU	European Union
EU-27	European Union including all current 27 member nations
GATT	General Agreement on Tariffs and Trade
GDP	Gross Domestic Product
GTAP	Global Trade Analysis Project
FTA	Free Trade Agreement
NLS	Non-Linear Least Squares
OECD	Organisation for Economic Co-operation and Development
OLS	Ordinary Least Squares
PPML	Poisson Pseudo-maximum Likelihood
QLME	Quasi-maximum Likelihood Estimation
RTA	Regional Trade Agreements
TUR	Turkey
USD	United States Dollar
WTO	World Trade Organization

1 Introduction

1.1 Why research Non-Tariff Barriers to Trade

Ever since David Ricardo came up with his "Law of Comparative Advantage" (Ricardo 1817) it has been a central argument for the establishment of free trade agreements around the world. It states that even if one of two countries is less efficient in the production of each of its goods than the other one, it will still gain from trade with the other country as long as the two differ in their relative efficiency of producing different goods.

Probably the most notable international free trade agreements were reached within the World Trade Organisation (WTO) and its predecessor, the General Agreement on Tariffs and Trade (GATT), which was founded in 1947. By 1994, the GATT had a total of 124 member countries (WTO 2012) that agreed to lower international tariffs on trade. For instance, between 1947 and 1994 the average tariff on industrial products traded between the members was lowered from 40% to 3.8% (Past et al. 2007, p. 6).

No longer able to apply tariffs, many nations resorted to an alternative way of impeding international trade in order to protect their less competitive industries, namely Non-Tariff Barriers to Trade (hereafter NTBs) (Past et al. 2007, p.3).

NTBs can be defined as "any measure (public or private) that causes internationally traded goods and services [...] to be allocated in such a way as to reduce potential real world income" (Baldwin 1970, p.5). While various ways of classifying NTBs can be found in literature, Baldwin (1970) divides them into twelve groups:

- Quotas and restrictive state-trading policies
- Export subsidies and taxes
- Discriminatory government and private procurement policies
- Selective indirect taxes

- Selective domestic subsidies
- Restrictive customs procedures
- Antidumping regulations
- Restrictive administrative and technical regulations
- Restrictive business practices
- Controls over foreign investment
- Restrictive immigration policies
- Selective monetary controls and discriminatory exchange-rate policies

The WTO prohibits the introduction or retention of NTBs (Past et al. 2007, p.15). However, proving the existence of an NTB is not easy (Past et al. 2007, p. 7). This is one of the reasons why there is a rising amount if international literature on how to detect and scale NTBs.

1.2 Structure of the Thesis

After this overview in part one on what NTBs are and how they can be measured in general, part two will deal with the border effect approach as a means of estimating NTBs in particular. In part three, I will apply the border effect approach to agricultural trade between Turkey and the EU, before drawing some conclusions in part 4.

1.3 Ways of capturing NTBs

1.3.1 The Price Gap Method

The method shows by how much NTBs within a country have lifted the domestic price of a good above the international price. This allows to take the "workings of policies" into account as well as to convert results into tariff equivalents. However, not only may price data availability be problematic, it is difficult to determine whether one of the prices is fully affected by an NTB whilst the other is completely unaffected. This method is sometimes called a handicraft, because it can literally be done manually with pen and paper. (Ferrantino 2006, p. 9.)

1.3.2 Price-based Econometric Methods

Price-based econometric methods extend the price-gap method to many countries and products at a time while taking systematic price differences into account, showing how much of a price difference may be attributable to NTBs. They enable us to compare how NTBs affect different countries or product groups. Price data unavailability as well as the method's incapability to make use of "product- and policy specific detail", which may cause the results to differ from those of a case specific analysis, as well as the influence of econometric specifications on results, are problematic. (Ferrantino 2006, p. 9.)

1.3.3 Quantity-based Econometric Methods

Data on traded quantities are not only better available internationally than price data, but also more standardised, which may make it possible to see how NTBs affect trade flows. Three types of models can be distinguished:

- Gravity models: explain trade by size of countries, distance between them and other factors
- Factor-content models: explain trade by different resource availability between countries
- Mixtures of the previous two

A significant amount of research is carried out to improve these methods. The non-includability of country- and product specific information and the influence of econometric specifications on results may be more problematic than with price-based methods. To convert results into tariff equivalents or price gaps, additional information and / or assumptions are required. (Ferrantino 2006, p. 10.)

NTBs are often introduced primarily to reduce trade flows, which lowers domestic supply and only secondarily leads to an increase in prices, along with a range of other factors that may influence prices. These other factors will not bias quantity-based methods (Ferrantino 2006, p. 21, point 64).

Therefore, I will apply a quantity-based approach and in particular a gravity model in this thesis when examining agricultural trade between Turkey and the EU.

1.3.4 Simulations Methods

Simulating the effect of changes in tariffs and other border barriers on trade, price and other economic variables can be done either in a partial (to focus on specific products or sectors) or general equilibrium setting. To simulate the effects of the introduction or removal of a NTB, a tariff equivalent (TEV) of the NTB must have been estimated by one of the above methods in order to implement it into the simulation. It is possible to perform sensitivity analyses to see which assumptions influence the simulation outcome by how much; simulations are also capable of explaining causal relationships. (Ferrantino 2006, p. 10)

1.4 The Gravity Equation in Physics and Economics

This thesis will focus on gravity models as a quantity-based econometric method to measure NTBs. In physics, the Newtonian gravity model predicts the force with which two objects will pull at each other by using the formula:

$$F = G\frac{m_1 m_2}{r^2} \qquad (1)$$

where: F: Absolute value of the gravitational force
G: Gravitational Constant
m_1, m_2: Masses of two globular objects
r: Distance between the centres of the two objects
G: Gravitational Constant
(Hammer et al. 2001)

Tinbergen (1962) was the first to apply the formula to predict trade flows between countries. In his work, F becomes the monetary measure of a trade flow between two countries, m_1 and m_2 represent the GDPs of the countries, and r is the distance between them.

While there is a variety of applications of the gravity model in economics, I will follow the development of the border effect approach as a particularly promising and researched way to capture the effect of NTBs.

2 The Border Effect Approach

A first attempt to apply the gravity equation to estimate the trade impeding effect of a border was carried out by McCallum (1995) when he compared Canadian interprovincial trade to international trade between Canada and the U.S. With this new methodology and his finding that without the border trade flows between Canada and the U.S. would be 2200% larger, he caused widespread interest in the topic and a large amount of related research to be carried out.

Improvements to the approach focused somewhat on the used data (McCallum did not take U.S. interstate trade into account), but mainly on the specification of the gravity equation and found still significant, if lower, border effects looking at the same data as McCallum.

The Border Effect Approach is particularly interesting when trying to quantify the effect of non-tariff barriers. If it was possible to get a consistent estimate of the total border effect, then deducting the known effect of tariffs from it would leave us with an estimate of the effects of non-tariff barriers.

Thus, chapter 2 will look into the original approach by McCallum and its most significant advancements by later contributions in order to obtain a consistent approach for the analysis of agricultural trade between Turkey and the EU.

2.1 The Original Approach by McCallum

In his 1995 paper "National Borders Matter: Canada-U.S. Regional Trade Patterns", McCallum conducts a widely noted application of the following gravity equation to examine the determinants of international trade patterns:

$$lnX_{ij} = a + b\ lny_i + \ c\ lny_i + \ d\ \ lndist_{ij} + \ e\ DUMMY + \ u_{ij} \qquad (2)$$

where

X_{ij}: Shipments from country i to country j

y_i, y_j: GDPs of country i and j

DUMMY: Dummy variable that takes the value one for intra-national and zero for international trade

u_{ij}: Error Term

As apparent from equation (2), McCallum has logarithmised it in order to enable a standard ordinary least squares (hereafter OLS) estimation. He uses the equation to compare 1988 data on trade between Canadian provinces to trade between Canadian provinces and U.S. states in order to show the effect of the U.S.-Canadian border. Notably, 1988 is the year that the FTA, a free trade agreement between the U.S. and Canada, was signed. McCallum assumes that FTA did not yet impact the effect of the border during the examined year. Data on interprovincial trade flows between all ten Canadian provinces as well as trade between those provinces and the 30 U.S. states that account for 90% of U.S.-Canadian trade are taken into account. This means that the author did not include intra-national trade flows between U.S. states, the potential effect of which will be discussed in section 2.2. This leads to a total of 690 observations, out of which 7 are zero-values, the logarithm of which cannot be taken, which is why McCallum does not include them in the estimation. The potential bias arising from this neglect of zero-values will be dealt with in section 2.3.

The equation is then estimated by OLS. Assuming that the border effect for Canada can be expressed as the exponential of the coefficient of DUMMY, it results that trade is expected to be an average of 22 times larger between two jurisdictions that are not separated by a border. McCallum also identifies a number of potential econometric problems to this approach. For one, he acknowledges the biasing effect heteroskedasticity may have on results. To test if it does, he estimates the gravity equation three more times, once by only using data from large jurisdictions with large GDP, once again by using all available data but weighing the regression towards jurisdictions with large GDP, and finally by using all data and substituting minimal trade flows for the zero-values. Also, he realises the problem that the dependent variable (exports) is a component of one of the regressors (GDP), the latter of which will thus be correlated to the error term. To find out about the disturbing effect of this, he estimates the gravity equation two more times, once while using the logarithm of population as instruments of GDP, and once by replacing the logarithms of GDPS with logarithms of population altogether. In none of these additional regressions do the results defer significantly from the original ones, from which McCallum concludes that neither heteroskedasticity nor the correlation of exports and the error term have lead to a biased estimate of the border effect. Furthermore, results also remain stable when the following aspects are incorporated into the model:

- Distance represented as logarithm, natural number or square of the natural number
- Province-specific constant terms (indicator of a province's overall exports) and province-specific coefficients (indicators of the degree to which each province's trade is biased towards exports to other provinces)
- Provinces' production structures (share of agriculture and manufacturing in GDP)
- Interaction term between DUMMY and the other explanatory variables, or the squares of y_i, y_j and *dist*

All in all, McCallum finds a significant hindering effect of the U.S.-Canadian border on trade flows.

2.2 Multilateral Resistance Terms

Anderson and van Wincoop (2003) argue that the paper of McCallum (1995) and related literature lack a theoretical foundation of the gravity equation, which has two negative implications: Firstly, an omitted variable bias can be expected and secondly, comparative static exercises, e.g. to show the effects of removing a trade barrier, cannot be conducted conclusively, because a countries resistance to trade with a bilateral partner also always depends on its resistance to trade with all other partners. The latter, however, is mostly the reason to estimate a gravity model in the first place.

The original gravity equation by Anderson 1979 is based on constant elasticity of substitution (CES) preferences and the differentiation of goods by region of origin. Anderson and van Wincoop (2003) were the first to manipulate the CES expenditure system in order to derive a gravity model from it. From this, three components of trade resistance can be derived:

- The bilateral trade barrier between i and j
- i's resistance to trade with all regions
- j's resistance to trade with all regions

I will now show how these components can be captured by the so-called Multilateral Resistance Terms (hereafter MRTs), and how these MRTs can be created from a theoretical derivation of the gravity equation.

2.2.1 Theoretical Derivation of the Gravity Equation

Feenstra (2002) shows how the gravity equation can be derived from a CES expenditure system: He points out that in the face of border effects, McCallum 's (1995) assumption that prices equalize across countries is no longer true and patterns of trade are more complex than reflected in his gravity equation. To deal with this, Feenstra (2002) develops his gravity equation from the assumed CES utility function:

$$U_j = \sum_{i=1}^{C} \sum_{k=1}^{N_i} (c_k^{ij})^{\frac{\sigma-1}{\sigma}} \qquad (3)$$

where U_j: Utility of consumers in country j

C: Number of countries in sample

N_i: Number of products produced by country i

c_k^{ij}: Exports from i to j of good k

σ: Elasticity of Substitution

To simplify this, the author adopts the "iceberg transportation cost" approach by Samuelson (1952):

$$p_{ij} = T_{ij}p_i \tag{4}$$

where T_{ij}: Units of a product that must be shipped from i to j in order for one unit

to arrive (the rest "melts" away due to transport cost)

p_i: Price for the product in country i

p_{ij}: Price consumers in j pay for the good from i

Transport cost then could be written as $t_{ij} = T_{ij} - 1$. When transport cost is equal for all varieties of a good, consumption will be equal for all products k=1,...,N_i in country j, so that

$$U_j = \sum_{i=1}^{C} N_i(c_{ij})^{\frac{\sigma-1}{\sigma}} \tag{5}$$

where c_{ij}: Consumption of all products from i in j

Consumers from j will maximize this utility function subject to their budget constraint:

$$Y_j = \sum_{i=1}^{C} N_i p_{ij} c_{ij} \tag{6}$$

where Y_j: Income (or GDP) in country j

From this maximization, the demand of each product is derived as:

$$c_{ij} = \left(\frac{p_{ij}}{p_j}\right)^{-\sigma}\left(\frac{Y_j}{P_j}\right) \tag{7}$$

where P_j is j's overall price index:

$$P_j = \left(\sum_{i=1}^{C} N_i (p_{ij})^{1-\sigma}\right)^{\frac{1}{1-\sigma}} \tag{8}$$

If we define the total value of exports from i to j as:

$$X_{ij} = N_{ij} p_{ij} c_{ij} \tag{9}$$

then it follows from (7) and (8):

$$X_{ij} = N_i Y_j \left(\frac{p_{ij}}{P_j}\right)^{1-\sigma} \qquad \text{"Theoretical Gravity Equation"} \tag{10}$$

The author summarizes three options of estimating this equation so that multilateral resistance is taken account of: The use of price index data, the use of estimated border effects as in Anderson and van Wincoop 2003 and the use of fixed effects, all of which will be presented in the following.

2.2.2 Use of Price Index Data

I follow Feenstra (2002) and, since the variable N_i in the gravity equation (10) is unobservable, we apply the zero-profit assumption to infer that the output of each firm in i, $\bar{y}$, is constant. Therefore, the GDP of country i can be calculated as:

$$Y_i = N_i \, p_i \, \bar{y} \tag{11}$$

or:

$$N_i = \frac{Y_i}{p_i \bar{y}} \tag{12}$$

Substituting this into the gravity equation (10) we get:

$$X_{ij} = \frac{Y_i Y_j}{p_i \bar{y}} \left(\frac{p_{ij}}{p_j} \right)^{1-\sigma} \tag{13}$$

Since $p_{ij} = T_{ij} p_i$, we can rewrite this as:

$$X_{ij} = \frac{Y_i Y_j}{{p_i}^{\sigma} \bar{y}} \left(\frac{T_{ij}}{P_j} \right)^{1-\sigma} \tag{14}$$

This can be transformed into the estimation equation by taking logarithms and first differences of variables:

$$\Delta \ln X_{ij} = \Delta \ln (Y_i Y_j) + (1-\sigma) \Delta \ln T_{ij} - \sigma \Delta \ln p_i + (\sigma - 1) \Delta \ln P_j \tag{15}$$

As a data source for the price indexes p_i and P_j, GDP deflators can be used.

There are two problems with this approach. Firstly, aggregate price indexes cannot really capture the full extent of cross-border transaction cost and the risk (money, time, currency). Secondly, price indexes refer to a certain base period for which the index is set to equal 100. This base period frequently differs from country to country, making indexes incomparable to each other. Therefore, an alternative approach is introduced:

2.2.3 Use of estimated Border Effects

This approach to estimating the gravity equation is the one originally introduced by Anderson and van Wincoop (2003). As described by Feenstra (2002), they work around the problem of incomparable price indexes by modeling p_{ij} as a function of p_i and trade costs, using the equation:

$$\ln T_{ij} = \tau_{ij} + \rho \ln d_{ij} + \varepsilon_{ij} \qquad \text{"}Estimated\ Border\ Effects\text{"}, (16)$$

where: T_{ij}: "Iceberg" transportation cost

d_{ij}: Distance between i and j

τ_{ij}: Any border effect related to exports from i to j other than distance

ε_{ij}: Random Error

If we substitute this back into the gravity equation (14), we will receive a set of equations where exports depend on τ_{ij} and ρ. However, those equations are not linear and thus difficult to estimate; therefore, the market clearing condition may be used to further simplify the gravity equation. The market clearing condition, assuming that output is greater than consumption due to "iceberg" transportation cost, is:

$$Y_i = \sum_{j=1}^{C} c_{ij} T_{ij} \qquad \text{"}Market\ Clearing\ Condition\text{"}, (17)$$

Multiplying this by $p_i = \frac{p_{ij}}{T_{ij}}$ (from (4)), we can rewrite:

$$p_i Y_i = \sum_{j=1}^{C} (p_{ij} c_{ij}) \qquad (18)$$

Assuming symmetric bilateral trade cost (i.e. $T_{ij} = T_{ji}$), the market clearing condition (17) can implicitly be solved as:

$$p_i = \frac{\left(\frac{s_i}{N_i}\right)^{\frac{1}{1-\sigma}}}{P_i} \qquad (19)$$

where: s_i: The share of i's GDP relative to the sum of GDPs of i and j,

i.e. $s_i = Y_i/(Y_i + Y_j)$

Multiplying this by T_{ij}, we get:

$$p_i T_{ij} = \tilde{p}_{ij} = (\frac{s_i}{N_i})^{\frac{1}{1-\sigma}} \frac{T_{ij}}{\tilde{P}_i} \qquad (20)$$

Substituting (20) into the price index (8) yields:

$$P_j^{\,1-\sigma} = \sum_{i=1}^{C} s_i \left(\frac{T_{ij}}{P_i}\right)^{1-\sigma} \tag{21}$$

This gives us the gravity equation:

$$X_{ij} = \left(\frac{Y_i Y_j}{Y_w}\right)\left(\frac{T_{ij}}{P_i P_j}\right)^{1-\sigma} \tag{22}$$

Due to the relationship expressed in (21), , $P_i$and P_j depend on the estimated border effect T_{ij} and can be called "Multilateral Resistance Terms". While they cannot be observed directly, they can be estimated using (21) together with formula (16) to solve for the estimated border effect.

In order to estimate this equation, the GDP terms may be moved to the left, equation (21) may be substituted for transportation cost, before taking natural logarithms:

$$\ln\left(\frac{X_{ij}}{Y_i Y_j}\right) = \rho(1-\sigma)\ln d_{ij} + (1-\sigma)\tau_{ij} + \ln(P_i)^{\sigma-1} + \ln\left(P_j\right)^{\sigma-1} + (1-\sigma)\varepsilon_{ij} \tag{23}$$

This equation needs to be estimated iteratively; while minimizing the sum of squared residuals, (16) must be applied to include the border effect at each iteration and these are used to solve for the multilateral resistance terms from (21). Also, it is necessary to be more explicit about the border effects $(1-\sigma)\tau_{ij}$ in (23): Replacing $(1-\sigma)\tau_{ij}$ with $\gamma(1-\delta_{ij})$ where δ_{ij} is the same dummy variable that McCallum 1995 used (i.e. unity for interprovincial trade and zero otherwise), and using α and γ as coefficients on distance and $(1-\delta_{ij})$, respectively , we can rewrite:

$$\ln\left(\frac{X_{ij}}{Y_i Y_j}\right) = \alpha\ln d_{ij} + \gamma\left(1-\delta_{ij}\right) + \ln P_i^{\,\sigma-1} + \ln P_j^{\,\sigma-1} + (1-\sigma)\varepsilon_{ij} \tag{24}$$

When interpreting the results of this estimation, a problem arises: Simply taking the exponent of γ and interpreting it as the border effect is no longer viable because a removal of the border would also affect the MRTs. A solution is to compare trade in presence (X_{ij}) and absence ($\overline{X_{ij}}$) of the border effect: If we say $\overline{P_i}^{\sigma-1}$ are the MRTs in absence of the border effect, calculated from formula (21), but obtaining T_{ij} in (16) as the logarithm of distance times its estimated coefficient only, take exponents of (24) and compare this equation with and without border effects, we get the ratio of trade in these two cases:

$$\frac{X_{ij}}{\overline{X_{ij}}} = \left[e^{(1-\delta_{ij})}\right] \frac{P_i^{\sigma-1} P_j^{\sigma-1}}{\overline{P_i}^{\sigma-1} \overline{P_j}^{\sigma-1}} \tag{25}$$

Applying this to the original data of McCallum 1995, Anderson and van Wincoop (2003) find intra-Canadian trade to be 4.3 times and intra-US trade to be 1.05 times larger due to the presence of the border than what they would be without it, whereas international trade is 0.41 times smaller. From this, they calculate intra-Canadian trade to be 4.3 / 0.41 = 10.5 times higher than cross-border trade; the analogous number for intra-US trade is 1.05 / 0.41 = 2.6. The average border effect can then be calculated as the geometric mean of the two border effects, i.e. $(10.5 * 2.6)^{1/2} = 5.2$. Feenstra (2002) points out that 5.2 is the exact same value one would obtain by taking the exponent of γ, the coefficient of the cross-border dummy variable, and proves mathematically that doing so is a completely valid way of inferring the average (over countries) impact of the border on intra-national relative to international trade.

One may wish to note that in order to do these calculations, it is necessary to assume a value for the elasticity of substitution, σ. Feenstra 2002 assumes it to take the value 5, but hints that Anderson and van Wincoop 2003 found it to be irrelevant if the value is altered between 2 and 20 in their sensitivity analysis.

In their original paper on gravity models using estimated border effects, Anderson and van Wincoop (2003) also argue that McCallum 's (1995) estimate of the border parameter for Canada is too large for two reasons:

Firstly, in the relatively small Canadian economy the border raises inter-province trade more relative to international trade than it raises inter-state trade in the U.S relative to international trade. With the U.S. being a large economy, international trade makes up a smaller proportion of total U.S. trade than it does of total Canadian trade.

Secondly, the omitted variable bias can be attributed to two sources:

(a) Estimation bias ("ordinary econometric emitted variable bias"): While in Anderson and van Wincoop 's (2003) paper the MRTs are calculated as

$$(1-\sigma)\ln b_{ij} - (1-\sigma)\ln P_i - (1-\sigma)\ln P_j \qquad (26)$$

where: b_{ij}: Border dummy that equals one for intra-national trade and zero for international trade

it is only a dummy variable that equals one for international trade flows in McCallum 's (1995) paper. Since the MRTs, however, are correlated with both distance and the dummy variable in his equation, McCallum 's (1995) estimation produces a biased estimate.

(b) Computation bias, resulting from comparative statics based on omitted terms: Even if McCallum's (1995) method would produce unbiased estimates of the coefficients of distance and the dummy variable, comparative statics based on these estimates would still be biased since MRTs will also change when a border effect is newly or no longer considered. This effect will inflate the border effect of Canada while reducing that of the U.S.

This demonstrates that when conducting the comparative statics experiment of eliminating a border, one must take into account its effect on multilateral resistance. It shows that the "the more resistant to trade with all others a region is, the more it is pushed into trading with a given bilateral partner" (Anderson 1979). Anderson and van Wincoop (2003) find that almost all the omitted variable bias can be attributed to the computation bias, whereas the estimation bias plays no significant role.

As seen, this method requires custom programming to perform the constrained minimization, and thus is tedious to conduct. A possible solution to this problem may be the use of fixed effects.

2.2.4 Use of Fixed Effects

As a solution to this, Feenstra (2002) suggests to, instead of calculating the MRTs in (17) by using (12) and applying T_{ij} (9), measure the MRTs as coefficients of source and destination region fixed effects, setting:

δ_1^i: Dummy variable, unity if i is the exporter, zero otherwise.
δ_2^j: Dummy variable, unity if j is the importer, zero otherwise.

This gives us the new gravity equation:

$$\ln(\frac{X_{ij}}{Y_i Y_j}) = \alpha \ln d_{ij} + \gamma(1 - \delta_{ij}) + \beta_1^i \delta_1^i + \beta_2^j \delta_2^j + (1 - \sigma)\varepsilon_{ij} \tag{27}$$

in which the coefficients $\beta_1^i = \ln P_i^{\sigma-1}$ and$\beta_2^j = \ln P_j^{\sigma-1}$ on the source and destination indicator variables estimate the multilateral indexes resistance.
Applying this to the McCallum (1995) data, the author interprets the exponential of γ as the average border effect and estimates a value of 4.7, which he views as reasonably close to the 5.2 calculated with the use of estimated border effects. It is also very close to the value of 4.8 which he receives when estimating the McCallum (1995) gravity equation but, unlike McCallum, includes intra-US trade in the data. This latter approach apparently corrects itself by overstating the border effect for Canada (15.7 instead of 10.5) and understating the effect for the US (1.49 instead of 2.56).

Feenstra (2002) concludes that the fixed effects approach, while being simple to implement, leads to consistent estimates of the border effect and may be preferred over the other two.

2.3 The Trouble with Heteroskedasticity – Why OLS-Estimation of Log-linearised Models is problematic

2.3.1 Jensen's Inequality and its Implications for Log-linearised Models

Jensen's Inequality states if $f: \mathbb{R} \longrightarrow \mathbb{R}$ is a convex function defined on $\mathbb{R}$ and the expected value of the dependent variable, $\mathrm{E}[|y|] < \infty$, it implies: $f[E(y|x)] \leq E[f(y)|x]$. (Wooldridge 2010, p. 31)

Santos Silva and Tenreyro (2010) argue that this implies $E(\ln y) \neq \ln E(y)$. According to them, with economic models like the gravity equation not holding with the accuracy of physical laws but on average only, they can only be used to calculate the (conditional) expected value of the dependent variable, i.e. $E[y_i|x]$. Therefore, the widely spread habit of estimating the gravity equation and, in fact, a multitude of econometric models in their log-linear form can lead to biased estimates. The authors also explain why this bias arises in the face of heteroskedasticity. They begin the derivation of this result by a general consideration of Constant Elasticity of Substitution (hereafter CES) models:

2.3.2 CES Models and Heteroskedasticity

Assuming y and x are linked by a CES model of the form $y_i = \exp(x_i\beta)$, which holds on average and has the error term $\varepsilon_i = y_i - E[y_i|x]$, the stochastic model can be formulated as:

$$y_i = \exp(x_i\beta) + \varepsilon_i \qquad (28)$$

where: $y_i \geq 0$ and $E[\varepsilon_i|x] = 0$

As an example of this, the multiplicative gravity equation could be rewritten as:

$$E(X_{ij}|Y_i, Y_j, D_{ij}) = \exp[\ln \alpha_0 + \alpha_1 \ln Y_i + \alpha_2 \ln Y_j + \alpha_3 \ln D_{ij}] \qquad (29)$$

where: X_{ij}: Trade flow from country i to j

Y_i, Y_j: GDP of country i and j, respectively

D_{ij}: Distance between i and j

The standard practice of log-linearising this model (28) and then estimating β by OLS does not lead to appropriate results for two reasons:

Firstly, observations of zero-values cannot be logarithmized and thus are generally either omitted or replaced by artificial minimal values, both of which will cause bias in results.

For the second reason, consider transforming the model (28) into:

$$y_i = \exp(x_i\beta) * \eta_i \qquad (30)$$

where:

$$\eta_i = 1 + \frac{\varepsilon_i}{\exp(x_i\beta)} \qquad (31)$$

and $E[\eta_i|x] = 1$. If $y_i > 0$, this model can be made linear:

$$\ln y_i = x_i\beta + \ln \eta_i \tag{32}$$

For the estimator of the slope parameters to be consistent, $E[\ln \eta_i \,|x]$ must not depend on x. Due to the relation expressed in (31), this will only be the case if $\varepsilon_i = \exp(x_i\beta) * v_i$, where v_i is a random variable statistically independent of x_i, so that η_i equals $1 + v_i$ and is therefore statistically independent of x_i.

The fact that trade can never assume a negative value has an important implication in this context: When the expected value of trade flow $E[y_i|x]$ approaches its lower bound, large positive deviations of the observed value from the expected value become unlikely since they cannot be offset by equally large negative deviations, which would be negative. The greater $E[y_i|x]$ becomes, the higher possible deviations can become. Therefore, the conditional variance of y_i, $V[y_i|x]$ will diminish with diminishing $E[y_i|x]$, i.e. the error term will be heteroskedastic.

In summary, the non-linear transformation of the dependent variable in (32) has a fundamental effect on the error term: The conditional expectation of $\ln \eta_i$ depends on the conditional distribution of η_i ; however, without strong restrictions on that distribution, it is impossible to infer the conditional expectation of y_i from the conditional expectation of $\ln y_i$, because $\ln \eta_i$ is correlated with the regressors. Thus, heteroskedasticity negatively impacts the consistency of an estimator.

Therefore, it has become clear why instead of the log-linear model, the non-linear model has to be estimated.

2.3.3 Finding an Appropriate Estimator for the Non-Linear Model

A non-linear least squares (hereafter NLS) estimator, as e.g. applied by Anderson and van Wincoop (2003), would be an asymptotically valid estimator for (6). Its incapability to adapt to patterns of heteroskedasticity, however, may make it inefficient because of the following:

An NLS estimator of β would be given as:

$$\hat{\beta} = \arg\min_{b} \sum_{i=1}^{n} [y_i - \exp(x_i b)]^2 \tag{33}$$

which implies the set of first-order conditions:

$$\sum_{i=1}^{n} [y_i - \exp(x_i \hat{\beta})] \exp(x_i \hat{\beta})\, x_i = 0 \tag{34}$$

This gives more weight to large values of $\exp(x_i \hat{\beta})$ since that is where the curvature of the conditional expectation is more pronounced. But, as we have seen, larger values also go along with a larger variance. Thus, the property of the NLS estimator of giving more weight to noisier observations may make it inefficient.

If the form of the expected conditional variance $V[y_i|x]$ was known, this problem could be solved by weighing the NLS estimator accordingly, but it isn't. That, in turn, could be solved by applying a nonparametric generalized least squares estimator, but that proves to be a very complex procedure. The authors therefore follow McCullagh and Nelder (1989) in applying a Poisson Pseudo-maximum Likelihood (PPML) estimator. Before showing its application in the gravity model by Santos Silva and Tenreyro (2010) in section 2.3.5., I will give a short explanation of this type of estimation in section 2.3.4.

2.3.4 Maximum Likelihood Estimation and Poisson Regressions

Maximum likelihood estimation aims to find estimates of the coefficients that make the observed data most likely to occur; i.e. it is assumed that the observed data is only a sample of all possible observations, and then those values of the coefficients that would make the observed data most likely to occur in a random sample are chosen. For this purpose, a function that explains the likelihood of the observed data depending on the estimated coefficients is created and maximised iteratively. In practice, it is generally more feasible to take the logarithm of that likelihood function, multiply it by minus one and then minimise it. (Purcell 2007)

Alternatively, a simplified form of the log-likelihood function may be used. In that case, the estimation is called pseudo- or quasi-maximum likelihood. (Gong and Samaniego 1981)

The PPML estimator employed by Santos Silva and Tenreyro (2006) applies pseudo-maximum likelihood estimator to Poisson distributed numbers.

A Poisson distribution predicts the likelihood of an integer, nonnegative count variable, such as the number of pieces of mail a person receives each day, taking a certain value, given that the mean of the assumed values is known and that assumed values do not depend on previously assumed values. (Bruce Brooks 2001)

A Poisson regression, then, models the likelihood of a dependent count variable assuming a certain value as a function of explanatory variables, and maximises that likelihood. It has the property of yielding consistent and asymptotically normal estimators for the explanatory variables' coefficients even if the dependent variable does not follow a Poisson distribution. Thus, when a Poisson regression is run on a dependent variable that may not be Poisson distributed, it can be called a quasi-maximum likelihood estimation (QMLE). (Wooldridge 2009, p. 597-598)

An alternative term for quasi-maximum likelihood estimation in this context is pseudo-maximum likelihood estimation. (Lindsay 1988)

2.3.5 Application of the PPML Estimator in the Gravity Model

Santos Silva and Tenreyro (2010) apply the PPML estimator in their gravity model: Based on the assumption that the conditional variance is proportional to the conditional mean, i.e. $E[y_i|x] \propto V[y_i|x]$, β can be estimated solving a set of first-order conditions:

$$\sum_{i=1}^{n}[y_i - \exp(x_i\hat{\beta})]x_i = 0 \qquad (35)$$

The PML estimator gives the same weight to all observations, because observations' additional information on curvature of the conditional mean is countered by their larger variance. This is a difference to the NLS estimator, which can be interpreted as a PML estimator assuming that $V[y_i|x] = const.$. While there is no further information available on heteroskedasticity, giving the same weight to all observations appears appropriate.

The authors find the estimator defined by equation (35) to be numerically equal to the PPML estimator. Further, they infer from equation (35) that the only prerequisite for the PPML estimator to be consistent is the correct specification of the conditional mean, i.e. $E[y_i|x] = \exp(x_i\beta)$. Therefore, even if the data is not Poisson distributed and y_i is not an integer, the estimator defined by equation (35) is still numerically equal to the PPML estimator.

This proves to be particularly handy since the PPML estimator can easily be calculated in standard econometric programmes such as STATA, the one used for this thesis.

In general, if it was known that $V[y_i|x]$ is a function of higher powers of $E[y_i|x]$, more efficient estimates could be achieved by weighing even less the large observations. In the case of trade data, however, the data of larger countries can be assumed to be of higher quality than that of smaller countries, which is why it is probably better to not weigh small observations even more.

The PPML estimator, then, appears to be a good compromise, since it doesn't weigh the large observations with their high variance as much as the NLS estimator, but also doesn't weigh the small observations with their measurement errors and lesser information on curvature too much.

2.4 The Problem of Endogeneity

As seen, significant research has been devoted to the improvement and further development of the border effect approach. It is seen as a reliable tool to illustrate the impact of borders on trade and applied in related studies (e.g. Chang and Hayakawa 2010, Olper and Raimondi 2008 and Winchester 2009).

And yet, Heinemeyer et al. (2008) find a systematic flaw to it, namely the problem of endogeneity. They argue not only may borders have an impact on trade flows, but trade flows may well have an influence on the creation or elimination of borders.
They see a problem with the general approach in literature such as that of McCallum (1995) of conducting a cross-sectional analysis, i.e. comparing trade flows between regions not separated by a border to trade flows between regions separated by a border. If it was true that borders might have been formed along preexisting patterns of trade that may in turn have been caused, for instance, by ethno-linguistic networks, the only way of consistently estimating the effect of a border would be to compare trade between the same pairs of regions before and after the establishment or elimination of a border between them. To do so, they compare trade flows in Europe before and after the reshaping of borders after world war one. They find that "most of the 1919 border changes followed a pattern of trade relations across the region that was clearly visible already before 1914" (p. 33/34), inferring that the effect of the actual borders is less than what a cross-sectional analysis would suggest.

While subsequent literature on applications of the border effect approach has yet to find a way of dealing with this, it should be kept in mind that the so-called border effect measured in the literature and in this thesis may not be entirely attributable to borders.

3 Non-Tariff Barriers to Agricultural Trade between Turkey and the EU: An Empirical Analysis

3.1 Aim and Approach of Analysis

In this empirical part of the thesis, I will conduct a cross-section analysis of agricultural trade between Turkey and the EU during the year 2007 using the border effect approach. In particular, I will use trade flow data from the United Nations Food and Agricultural Organisation (hereafter FAO). With the related literature generally employing other data sources, the reader may find it interesting to see the results produced by applying this source. Furthermore, I aim to demonstrate the effect which aggregation and pooling of trade flow data has on results. Therefore, I will first analyse data on three single agricultural sectors (namely fruit, nuts and vegetables), in order to then run two more regressions for pooled (i.e. the single sector data sets attached to each other) and aggregated (i.e. the trade flows of fruit, nuts and vegetables between two given countries are summed up) data. The resulting estimates of border effects will be converted into ad-valorem tariff equivalents (hereafter AVEs) that will ensure comparability to related studies and could in theory be divided into the effects of actual tariffs and other effects including NTBs.

As seen in section 2.4., a cross-section analysis of intra- and international trade flows using the border effect approach will suffer from the problem of endogeneity, i.e. the fact that pre-existing patterns of trade flows may have influenced the creation or elimination of national borders, though the extent of this problem could only be measured using panel data on trading countries between which a border is erected or eliminated during the analysed time period. Yet, while the dimension of this problem remains unclear[1] and a viable alternative not suffering from the same problem is not available, the border effect approach remains the method most applied by up-to-date literature on the estimation of NTBs. As a consequence, by

[1] While Heinemeyer et al. (2008) could estimate the extent to which borders are impacted by preexisting patterns of trade in post-world-war-one Europe, they were able to do so because of the extensive reshaping of borders during that time. This thesis and most studies applying the border effect approach to modern day issues, however, concern trade across regions where borders are not created or eliminated.

applying the border effect approach one ensures the comparability of results to related literature.

Using the statistical software package STATA (StataCorp 2009), I will include Turkey, the EU as well as all OECD countries and six major agricultural traders, namely Brazil, China, India, Indonesia, Russia and South Africa in the sample, adding up to a total of 46 countries. While the estimation would be most accurate if all countries in the world were analyzed, I attempt to cover the most important agricultural traders while keeping sample size to a computationally feasible level.

3.2 Applied Gravity Model

Based on the options presented in Feenstra (2002) and discussed in section 2.2 (Multilateral Resistance Terms), I decide to capture the MRTs by means of applying the fixed effects approach in my model. This approach is simple to implement and has the capability of capturing country-specific parameters such as GDP, production and consumption in the fixed effect dummy variables, thus avoiding the need to retrieve that data. Thus, the following equation evolves:

$$\begin{aligned} Exports = \; & \exp(\beta_1 + \beta_2\, contig + \beta_3\, comlang\_ethno + \beta_4 \ln distw \\ & + \beta_5 colony + \beta_6\, RTA + \beta_7\, landlocked \\ & + \beta_8 BORDER_{EU-TUR} + \beta_9\, BORDER_{TUR-EU} \\ & + \beta_{10}\, BORDER_{EU} + \beta_{11} BORDER_{Other} + \beta_x ALPHA) \end{aligned} \qquad (36)$$

where *contig* (equals one if reporter and partner share a border, otherwise zero), *comlang_ethno* (equals one if a language is spoken by at least nine percent of population in each country, otherwise zero), *colony* (equals one if reporter and partner have a colonial relationship, otherwise zero) and *RTA* (equals one if reporter and partner have a regional trade agreement, otherwise zero) are dummy variables. *distw* represents the bilateral distance between trading countries, calculated as the population-weighted average of distances between major cities in these countries. *landlocked* takes the value one if either exporter or importer of a trade flow does not have access to the sea and two if neither of them does, otherwise it equals zero. The

Border variables are dummies that take the value one if a trade flow crosses the respective border (from the EU to Turkey, vice versa, an intra-EU border, or any other border, respectively) or zero otherwise. Finally, a number of dummy variables, all named beginning with *alpha*, capturing Exporter-/Importer- and/or sector-specific effects as a means of accounting for GDP, production and consumption in the respective countries as well as sector characteristics without gathering data on them. However, as different *Alpha*-Dummies have to be introduced for different estimations, they will be explained in detail in section 3.4. (Estimation).

Following Santos Silva and Tenreyro (2010), I will estimate the equation using the PPML estimator.

As a means of comparison, the equation will also be estimated using OLS, however, for the OLS estimation to be possible it will be necessary to use the natural logarithm of exports. Since a significant number of trade flow observations equal zero, which cannot be transformed into a natural logarithm, those zero-values will be substituted by a minimal value (one), which solves that problem but leads to a systematic bias of results.

The estimated border coefficients will then be converted into ad-valorem tariff equivalents.

3.3 Data

Taking 46 countries into account requires retrieving data on 46x45 = 2,070 international and 46 intra-national trade flows, i.e. a total of 2116 observations for each analysed sector. Data on international trade flows of single fruit, nut and vegetable products is taken from FAOSTAT (FAO 2012) and then aggregated into those three sectors. As for the intra-national data, I follow the wide-spread practice (compare e.g. Chen 2004, Olper and Raimondi 2008, Winchester 2009*)* based on Wei (1996) of calculating a country's "exports to self" as that country' production minus its exports of a specific product or product group. For this, I retrieve data from FAOSTAT on export value, export quantity and production quantity, each in aggregated form for the entire sectors fruit, nuts and vegetables. From this, I calculate the average price of each sector's products as the fraction of export value over export quantity, and then calculate the "exports to self" as the difference between production quantity and export quantity, multiplied by the price.

The variables *contig*, *comlang_ethno*, *distw*, *colony* and *RTA* are downloaded from the *"Centre d'Etudes Prospectives et d'Informations Internationales"* (hereafter CEPII) (Head et al. 2010) for international trade flows. For intranational data , I set *contig*, *comlang_ethno*, *colony* and *RTA* to equal one, since intranational trade is generally not obstructed by distance between countries (*contig*), language differences (*comlang_ethno*), lack of bilateral relations (*colony*) or tariffs *(RTA)*. *distw* for intra-national trade is calculated analogously to international trade by CEPII.

I create the variable *landlocked* as well as the *Border*-dummies and all *Alpha*-dummies myself.

3.4 Estimation and Results

3.4.1 Single sectors estimation using Importer-Exporter-Dummies

First, I estimate the gravity model for the three data sets for the sectors fruit, vegetables and nuts with the mentioned 2116 observations each. To capture GDP, production, consumption and other country-specific effects, each data set is fitted with Country-Importer / Exporter dummies, named after the scheme *alpha_country_function*; e.g. *alpha_HUN_imp* would equal one if Hungary was the importer of a trade flow and zero otherwise, whereas *alpha_CHE_exp* would equal one if Switzerland was the exporter of a trade flow and zero otherwise. Thus, there is a total of 46x2=92 *alpha*-variables in each data set. As mentioned, I also compare the results of the PPML estimation to those of an OLS method to see if results do differ as suggested by Santos Silva and Tenreyro (2006). Also, I conduct chi-square test on the significance of the group of country-dummies as a whole. The results of these estimations can be found in table (1).

Table 1: Results of Single Sector PPML and OLS Estimations

	Fruit		Nuts		Vegetables	
Sum of analysed trade flows	119 Bill. USD		10.6 Bill. USD		95.9 Bill. USD	
Estimator	**PPML**	**OLS**	**PPML**	**OLS**	**PPML**	**OLS**
R^2		.6813		.6272		.7033
Pseudo-R^2	.8927		.8788		.9640	
contig	.4194*	-.0312	-.3289	1.212*	.6592***	.7895
comlang_ethno	.4811*	-.1535	.8311**	.5740	.7042***	.3446
ln_distw	-.6512***	-1.976***	-1.175***	-	-1.021**	-2.51***
colony	-.1626	.0415	-1.134**	2.26***	-.8163***	1.620**
RTA	1.132***	1.618***	.0108	-.0869	1.905**	1.702***
landlocked	-.2815	-1.194	1.007	.8158	-.6239**	.9358
				2.527		
border_EU_TUR	-3.807***	-.6808	-.7618	3.980	-3.964**	1.661
border_TUR_EU	-1.587***	.1132	-.0974	1.614	-2.399**	2.828
border_EU	-1.067*	.8002	.2808	3.495	-1.0516*	3.653**
border_other	-.6136	.1699	-.2598	1.838	-.6954*	2.048
Alpha-Variables	***	***	***	***	***	***

** Indicates significance on 5% level; ** indicates significance on 1% level; *** indicates significance on 0.1% level; significance of all alpha-variables in each regression was tested using Chi-Square test; estimates rounded to four valid digits;*

Source: *Author's own calculations*

The R^2 values of the OLS regressions and the Pseudo-R^2 indicate a high goodness-of-fit of all six regressions. The PPML estimation of the fruit and vegetables sectors show a significant trade facilitating effect of contiguity, common language and RTAs. In the vegetables sector, PPML estimation indicates a significant trade impeding effect of colonial relationships and being landlocked. In both sectors, the significant border barrier for exports from the EU to Turkey is higher than for exports from Turkey to the EU. As one might expect, the border barrier for intra-EU trade is lower yet and also significant. All other borders, however, are estimated to have an even lower trade impeding effect, but that effect is not statistically significant in the fruit sector and only significant on the 5% level in the vegetables sector.

The PPML estimates for the nuts sector somewhat differ in scale, sign and significance. Since this sector only accounts for an analysed trade flow volume of 10.9 billion USD, one may doubt the explanatory power of this regression.

As for the OLS estimates, they differ widely between sectors, show hardly any resemblance to the PPML estimations and very few of them are statistically significant. With the obvious weakness of OLS estimation, I will only use the PPML method for the pooled and aggregated data.

In all single-sector regressions, the alpha-dummies are as a whole significant on the 0.1% level.

3.4.2 Pooled and aggregated Regression using PPML

In order to see the effects a pooling or aggregation of data may have on results, I run two more estimations.

For the pooled data (i.e. data on the three sectors attached to each other) it would be most accurate to generate one *Alpha*-dummy for each exporter and each importer for each sector following the scheme *alpha_country_function_sector*, so that e.g. *alpha_TUR_exp_nuts* equals one if Turkey is the exporter of a trade flow of nuts and zero otherwise. This would lead to the introduction of 46x2x3 = 276 *alpha*-dummies. With each sector contributing 2116 trade flows, a total of 3x2116 = 6348 observations would be covered. However, when regressing this model in the STATA software, iterations seeking to maximise the log-likelihood function do not converge.

Therefore, I resort to two alternative approaches:

- Using pooled data, but applying one set of dummies capturing countries and their function after the scheme *alpha_country_function* and adding a separate set of dummies capturing the sector following the scheme *alpha_sector*. As explained, the pooled data covers 6348 observations. The separation of the importer- / exporter dummies and sector dummies has the disadvantage of not capturing effects that are specific to a sector in a particular country and may lead to somewhat less reliable results.

- Using aggregated data, i.e. summing up the three trade flows of fruit, nuts and vegetables for each country pair, thus dealing with 2116 observations. This requires the use of exporter- / importer dummies following the scheme *alpha_country_function* like in the sector regressions. This has the disadvantage of not capturing any sector-specific effects.

As discussed, both alternatives are estimated using PPML. Their results are compared in table (2).

Notably, the estimates themselves do not differ between the two approaches, only their significances do. This is because no sector dummies were applied in the aggregated regression, leaving it with a somewhat lower explanatory power.

Table 2: Results of Pooled an Aggregated PPML Regressions

	Pooled with country-dummies and sector-dummies	Aggregated with Importer- / Exporter-dummies
Pseudo R^2	0.8836	0.9287
contig	.430944**	.430944**
comlang_ethno	.6272121**	.6272121**
ln_distw	-.7743738***	-.7743738***
colony	-.4090383	-.4090383
RTA	1.269863***	1.269863***
landlocked	-.3995831**	-.3995831*
border_EU_TUR	-3.690269***	-3.690269***
border_TUR_EU	-1.421702***	-1.421702***
border_EU	-1.047072**	-1.047072**
border_other	-.5792616*	-.5792616
Alpha-Variables	***	***

** Indicates significance on 5% level; ** indicates significance on 1% level; *** indicates significance on 0.1% level*

Source: *Author's own calculations*

After pooling or aggregating the data, contiguity, common language and RTAs still show significant positive effects that lie between the PPML estimates of the fruit and vegetable sector in their magnitude. The same is true for the significant negative effect of weighted distance and the landlocked variable. Colonial ties remain with a negative but now insignificant estimate. As for the border coefficients, estimates for border_EU_TUR, border_TUR_EU and border_other closely resemble those of the fruit and vegetables single sectors PPML estimation in magnitude; border_EU_TUR and border TUR_EU are significant on the 0.1% level, while border_other is significant on the 5% level in the pooled regression and not significant in the aggregated one. The alpha-dummies, as in the single-sector regressions, are as a whole significant on the 0.1% level.

3.4.3 Comparison of aggregated / pooled regression results with literature

Befus et al. (2012) estimate effects of the EU, EU-TUR and TUR-EU borders for, amongst others, an aggregated Agro-Food Sector that includes only fruit, nuts and vegetables and thus resembles the aggregated and pooled regressions conducted in this thesis well. Their data originates from version 8 of the Global Trade Analysis Project (hereafter GTAP) data base, except for the data on distance, contiguity, common language and colonial ties, which they retrieve from CEPII as is done in this thesis. Another similarity is their calculation of intra-national trade, which they, as myself, calculate as "exports to self" following the approach of Wei (1996).

Applying the gravity equation specified in section 3.2 of this thesis to the data used in the paper by Befus et al. (2012) yields the estimates represented in table (3).

In both this thesis and the paper by Befus et al. (2012), distance, being landlocked have a significant negative, contiguity, common language and RTAs a significant positive impact on trade. Colonial ties are estimated to be insignificant in both studies. As for the border effects, all of them are significant in both studies but vary somewhat in extent. Notably, Befus et al. (2012) estimate trade flows from the EU to Turkey to face a higher border barrier than those from Turkey, which is again consistent with the results from section 3.4.2.

Table 3: Comparison of Pooled Regression Results

Coefficient	Estimates from section 3.4.2	Estimates by Befus et al. (2012)
ln_distw	-.7743738**	-1.126***
landlocked	-0.3995831**	-1.171***
contig	0.430994**	.34342*
comlang_ethno	.6272121**	1.1748***
colony	-0.4090383	-0.24237
RTA	1.269863**	1.1617***
border_EU	-1.047072**	-0.74686**
border_EU_TUR	-3.690269**	-3.7766***
border_TUR_EU	-1.421702**	-2.8352***
border_other	-0.5792616*	2.3181***

** Indicates significance on 5% level; ** indicates significance on 1% level; *** indicates significance on 0.1% level;*

Source: *Author's own calculations*

3.5 Calculation of AVEs

Following Olper and Raimondi (2008), I convert the above estimated border coefficients into ad-valorem tariff equivalents (hereafter AVEs). As apparent from the theoretically derived gravity equation as represented by formula (23), our border estimates are in fact estimates of $(1-\sigma)ln\,\tau_{ij}$. According to Olper and Raimondi (2008), τ_{ij} equals one plus the AVE of the trade barriers related to the border, so that:

$$border_{ij} = (1 - \sigma_{ij}) \ln(1 + AVE) \quad (37)$$

Thus, the AVEs can be calculated as:

$$AVE = \exp\left[\frac{border_{ij}}{1 - \sigma_{ij}}\right] - 1 \quad (38)$$

As apparent from formula (38), the choice of a realistic elasticity of substitution is crucial to the calculation of appropriate AVEs. As Olper and Raimondi (2008) point out though, there is no good source for elasticity values, especially since these may vary over different countries and products. Therefore, I follow them in applying three alternative values (3, 5 and 7) which are frequently used in related literature. The results of these calculations are displayed in table (4).

Table 4: Implied Ad-valorem Equivalents of Border Barriers (%)

	Fruit (PPML)			Nuts (PPML)			Vegetables (PPML)			Pooled / Aggregated		
σ	3	5	7	3	5	7	3	5	7	3	5	7
EU	36	17	11	14	7	4	42	19	12	34	16	10
EU - TUR	571	159	89	46	21	14	626	169	94	533	152	85
TUR - EU	121	49	30	5	2	2	232	82	49	104	43	27

Source: *Author's own calculations*

Maybe the most immediate result of this calculation is the influence of the elasticity of substitution. The AVEs calculated for $\sigma = 3$ are two to six times higher than the ones calculated for $\sigma = 7$. Therefore, the importance of applying a reliable measure of σ when calculating AVEs cannot be stressed enough. While this effect can be explained mathematically by formula (38), it can also be depicted as a result of consumer behaviour: The less consumers of a country are willing to replace domestic products by foreign ones, i.e. the lower their elasticity of substitution, the harder it will be for foreign products to cross the border into that country, leading to a higher implied AVE. Looking in particular at the AVEs implied by the pooled and aggregated regressions and $\sigma = 5$ as an average value, intra-EU trade faces an average border barrier AVE of 30%. Since there are language and cultural differences as well as a number of landlocked countries, this appears plausible even within the common market area of the EU. Imports from Turkey into the EU face an only slightly higher AVE of 43%, whereas exports from the EU into Turkey are confronted with an AVE of 152%. The result that trade flows of agricultural products from the EU to Turkey face higher AVEs than vice versa is consistent with related literature (compare Befus et al. 2012)

While these values are higher for vegetables (19%, 82% and 169 %, respectively) than for the pooled / aggregated products, they are lower for fruit (17%, 49% and 159%, respectively) and lower yet for nuts (7%, 2% and 21%, respectively); however, one should keep in mind that the regression on nuts with a total analysed trade flow volume of only 10.6 billion USD may not be reliable.

Following Olper and Raimondi (2008), I also calculate the part of each implied AVE that cannot be explained by a tariff. For this purpose, I subtract the reported tariff rate from the total implied AVEs. These unexplained parts of the AVEs reflect NTBs, but may well be impacted by other trade impeding phenomena such as for instance consumer preferences, so that the actual scope of NTBs still cannot be deduced.

To comply with the Harmonized Commodity and Coding System applied by the source of reported tariff rates (ITC 2012), I calculate a single implied AVE for fruit and nuts by weighing the two implied AVEs of these sectors by their trade volume across each analysed border. The calculations behind this weighting can be found in appendix 1. The unexplained parts of the AVEs are presented in table (4). As apparent, the share of tariff rates in total implied AVEs depends, again, largely on the assumed elasticity of substitution.

Table 5: Unexplained Part of Implied AVEs

Fruit and Nuts

Border	Weighted Applied Tariff (%) *	$\sigma = 3$		$\sigma = 5$		$\sigma = 7$	
		Weighted Total Implied AVE (%) [1]	Unexplained part of AVE (%) **	Weighted Total Implied AVE (%) [1]	Unexplained part of AVE (%) **	Weighted Total Implied AVE (%) [1]	Unexplained part of AVE (%) **
Intra-EU	0	34.82	34.82	16.46	16.46	10.63	10.63
EU-TUR	65.1	434.05	368.95	123.06	57.96	69.48	4.38
TUR-EU	3.5	64.74	61.24	26.21	22.71	16.42	12.92

Vegetables

Border	Weighted Applied Tariff (%) *	$\sigma = 3$		$\sigma = 5$		$\sigma = 7$	
		Total Implied AVE (%) **	Unexplained part of AVE (%) **	Total Implied AVE (%)	Unexplained part of AVE (%) **	Total Implied AVE (%) **	Unexplained part of AVE (%) **
Intra-EU	0	42	42	19	19	12	12
EU-TUR	25.1	626	600.9	169	143.9	94	68.9
TUR-EU	5.6	232	226.4	82	76.4	49	43.4

1 Total implied AVEs from table (3) for fruit and nuts, weighted by share of trade flows across each border (for calculation, see appendix 1)

* ***Source:** ITC 2012*

** ***Source:** Author's own calculations*

4 Concluding Remarks

During the continuous reduction of tariffs on international trade within GATT and the WTO over the last decades, many nations around the world have recognised NTBs as an alternative tool by which they continue established protectionist policies. This has left modern trade policy analysis with no other option than to investigate ways of identifying and quantifying those NTBs.

In this context, the border effect approach as an application of the gravity equation for trade has established itself as the workhorse of scientific literature. It can be based on readily available data on international trade flows and results can easily be compared to related literature. Some of the challenges one faces when conducting this approach are the choice of an appropriate way to capture MRTs as well as a consistent estimation method. Recent findings, however, have focused on the endogeneity problem of the border effect approach, i.e. the fact that not only do borders affect trade flows, but patterns of trade may also impact the creation or elimination of borders. A reliable way of measuring the exact extent of this problem is yet to be found.

Applying the border effect approach to agricultural trade of fruit, nuts and vegetables between Turkey and the EU, this thesis has quantified effects of intra-EU and the EU-Turkey border. In particular, it was found that fruit and vegetables face a significantly higher border barrier when exported from the EU to Turkey than vice versa. A pooling and aggregation of these three sectors lead to more consistent estimates than single sector estimation and shed some light on the importance of the choice of country- and sector-specific dummy variables when applying fixed effects.

The conversion of border coefficient estimates from the border effect approach into AVEs brought to light the importance of a realistic choice of the elasticity of substitution when quantifying NTBs. The absence of a good source on these elasticities severely hampers the efforts to separate effects of tariffs from those of other measures such as NTBs and calls for more research on the topic.

5 References

ANDERSON, J. E.(1979). A Theoretical Foundation for the Gravity Equation. American Economic Review 69(1): pp. 106-116.

ANDERSON, J. E. and VAN WINCOOP, E.(2003). Gravity with Gravitas: A Solution to the Border Puzzle. American Economic Review 93(1): pp. 170-192.

BALDWIN, R. E. (1970): Nontariff Distortions of International Trade. Brookings Institution, Washington D.C.

BEFUS, T., BROCKMEIER, M. and BEKTASOGLU, B. (2012): Comparing Gravity Models Specifications to Estimate NTBs Using the GTAP Framework. Paper presented at the Global Trade Analysis Project (GTAP) 15th Annual Conference, Geneva, Switzerland, June 27-29, 2012. GTAP Resource #3910.

BRUCE BROOKS, E. (2001): Statistics: The Poisson Distribution. Available from: http://www.umass.edu/wsp/statistics/lessons/poisson/index.html (Retrieved October 12, 2012).

CHANG, K.-I. and HAYAKAWA, K.(2010). Border Barriers in Agricultural Trade and the Impact of Their Elimination: Evidence from East Asia. Developing Economies 48(2): pp. 232-246.

CHEN, N.(2004). Intra-national versus international trade in the European Union: why do national borders matter? Journal of International Economics 63(1): pp. 93-118.

FAO (2012): FAOSTAT. Food and Agricultural Organisation of the United Nations. Available from: http://faostat.fao.org (Retrieved October 15, 2012).

FEENSTRA, R. C.(2002). Border Effects and the Gravity Equation: Consistent Methods for Estimation. Scottish Journal of Political Economy 49(5): pp. 491-506.

FERRANTINO, M. (2006): Quantifying the Trade and Economic Effects of Non-Tariff Measures.

GONG, G. and SAMANIEGO, F. J.(1981). Pseudo Maximum Likelihood Estimation: Theory and Applications. The Annals of Statistics Vol. 9(No. 4): pp. 861-869.

HAMMER, A., HAMMER, H. and HAMMER, K. (2001): Physikalische Formeln und Tabellen. J. Lindauer Verlag (Schaefer), München.

HEAD, K., MAYER, T. and RIES, J. (2010): The CEPII Gravity Dataset. Centre d'Etudes Prospectives et d'Informations Internationales (CEPII). Available from: http://www.cepii.fr/anglaisgraph/bdd/gravity.asp (Retrieved September 15, 2012).

HEINEMEYER, H.-C., SCHULZE, M.-S. and WOLF, N. (2008): Endogenous Borders? The Effects of New Borders on Trade in Central Europe 1885-1933. CEPR Discussion Paper No. DP6909. Centre for Economic Policy Research (CEPR).

ITC (2012): Market Access Map. International Trade Center (ITC). Available from: http://www.macmap.org (Retrieved October 20, 2012).

LINDSAY, B. G.(1988). Composite Likelihood Methods. Contemporary Mathematics 80: pp. 221-239.

MCCALLUM, J.(1995). National Borders Matter: Canada-U.S. Regional Trade Patterns. American Economic Review 85 (3): pp. 615-23.

MCCULLAGH, P. and NELDER, J. A. (1989): Generalized Linear Models. Second Edition. Chapman and Hall, London.

OLPER, A. and RAIMONDI, V.(2008). Agricultural market integration in the OECD: A gravity-border effect approach. Food Policy 33(2): pp. 165-175.

PAST, H., SCHROTT, S., SPENGLER, J. and STOWASSER, C. (2007): Nicht-tarifäre Handelshemmnisse immer wichtiger für die Handelspolitik. Wirtschaftskammer Österreich (WKÖ), Wien, Österreich.

PURCELL, S. (2007): Maximum Likelihood Estimation. Available from: http://statgen.iop.kcl.ac.uk/bgim/mle/sslike_1.html (Retrieved October 15, 2012).

RICARDO, D. (1817): On the Principles of Political Economy and Taxation. John Murray, London.

SAMUELSON, P. A.(1952). The transfer problem and transport costs: the terms of trade when impediments are absent. Economic Journal 62: pp. 278-304.

SANTOS SILVA, J. M. C. and TENREYRO, S.(2006). The Log of Gravity. Review of Economics and Statistics 88(4): pp. 641-658.

STATACORP (2009): Stata Statistical Software: Release 11.1, Special Edition. StataCorp LP, College Station, Texas, USA.

TINBERGEN, J. (1962): Shaping the World Economy; Suggestions for an International Economic Policy. Twentieth Century Fund, New York.

WEI, S.-J.(1996). Intra-National versus International Trade: How Stubborn are Nations in Global Integration? National Bureau of Economic Research Working Paper Series No. 5531: pp.

WINCHESTER, N.(2009). Is There a Dirty Little Secret? Non-tariff Barriers and the Gains from Trade. Journal of Policy Modelling 31(6): pp. 819-834.

WOOLDRIDGE, J. M. (2009): Introductory econometrics. Fourth Edition,International Student Edition. South-Western Cengage Learning, Mason, Ohio.

WOOLDRIDGE, J. M. (2010): Econometric Analysis of Cross Section and Panel Data. Second Edition. MIT Press, Cambridge, Massachusetts, USA and London, UK.

WTO. (2012): The 128 countries that had signed GATT by 1994. Available from: http://www.wto.org/english/thewto_e/gattmem_e.htm (Retrieved 15.08.2012).

Appendix: Calculation of Weighted AVEs

For Intra-EU trade:

Trade flow fruit: $4.7 * 10^{10}$
Trade flow nuts: $0.266 * 10^{10}$

Share of fruit: 4.7 / (4.7+0.266)=.94643576
Share of nuts: .266/(4.7+0.266)=.05356424

Total implied AVE fruit (ES 3):36
Total implied AVE nuts (ES 3):14
Weighted AVE (ES 3): 36 * 0.94643576 + 14 * 0.05356424 = **34.821586 %**

Total implied AVE fruit (ES 5):17
Total implied AVE nuts (ES 5):7
Weighted AVE (ES 5): 17 * 0.94643576 + 7 * 0.05356424 = **16.464358 %**

Total implied AVE fruit (ES 7):11
Total implied AVE nuts (ES 7): 4
Weighted AVE (ES 7): 11 * 0.94643576 + 4 * 0.05356424 = **10.62505%**

For trade flows from the EU to Turkey:

Trade flow fruit: $5.99 * 10^{7}$
Trade flow nuts: $2.17 * 10^{7}$

Share of fruit: .73859433
Share of nuts: .2675709

Total implied AVE fruit (ES 3):571
Total implied AVE nuts (ES 3): 46
Weighted AVE (ES 3): 571 * .73859433 + 46 * .2675709 = **434.04562%**

Total implied AVE fruit (ES 5): 159
Total implied AVE nuts (ES 5):21
Weighted AVE (ES 5): 159 * .73859433 + 21 * .2675709 = **123.05549%**

Total implied AVE fruit (ES 7):89
Total implied AVE nuts (ES 7):14
Weighted AVE (ES 7): 89 * .73859433 + 14 * .2675709 = **69.480888%**

For trade flows from Turkey to the EU:

Trade flow fruit: $8.91 * 10^{8}$
Trade flow nuts: $8.39 * 10^{8}$

Share of fruit: .5150289
Share of nuts: .4849711

Total implied AVE fruit (ES 3):121
Total implied AVE nuts (ES 3):5
Weighted AVE (ES 3): 121*.5150289+5*.4849711 = **64.743352%**

Total implied AVE fruit (ES 5):49
Total implied AVE nuts (ES 5):2
Weighted AVE (ES 5): 49*.5150289+2*.4849711 = **26.206358%**

Total implied AVE fruit (ES 7):30
Total implied AVE nuts (ES 7):2
Weighted AVE (ES 7): 30*.5150289+2*.4849711 = **16.420809%**

www.ingramcontent.com/pod-product-compliance
Lightning Source LLC
LaVergne TN
LVHW102228300926
849160LV00005B/72